THE YES OF THE HEART

Faith, Hope & Love Songs
BY
RUSTY EDWARDS

Code No. 776

Hope Publishing Company
CAROL STREAM · IL 60188

FOREWORD

Religion and music are very closely connected. Every person's desire to improve their life and the lives of others shows itself through in the pursuit of religion and art. Our basic "right" to our freedom to think and create the beauty we see becomes a responsibility to actually use this basic capacity.

To create something beautiful for others to enjoy and have is the greatest feeling there is. If this were the only activity that we all ever engaged in, we would have a very sane, beautiful, and peaceful world.

Rusty has wonderfully utilized his ability to create something beautiful with **The Yes of the Heart.**

Even though Rusty and I are members of different religious groups, we share the idea that the freedom to believe is as basic as the freedom to create. And I'm sure that this spirit of freedom and creation will be enhanced by **The Yes of the Heart.**

Chick Corea
Los Angeles, California
October, 1992

INTRODUCTION

My first encounter with the work of The Rev. Dr. Howard Milton Edwards, III was in 1983 when the 28-year-old was an M. Div. candidate at Luther Northwestern Seminary in St. Paul, Minnesota. He had already provided the music for a folio of hymn texts by poet Gracia Grindal. Just nine hymns appeared in the little booklet entitled **SINGING THE STORY,** but the consistent quality of the texts and tunes was immediately obvious.

The following year we selected "To a Maid Engaged to Joseph" to his hymn tune *Annunciation* for our **HYMNAL SUPPLEMENT** which contained 130 new hymns. Most of the selections in that book were from the British exponents of the "Hymn Explosion" and sixty-two of the titles were the work of just four hymnwriters—F. Pratt Green, Fred Kaan, Timothy Dudley-Smith, and Brian Wren—who, at that time, clearly dominated the scene. However, as indicated, we did find room for a few new expressions from American authors and composers. This marked the first appearance of a Rusty Edwards (the name by which he prefers to be identified as a hymnwriter) tune in a commercially produced hymnal although, at that time, he was still using his full given name.

After graduation, Rusty became Assistant Pastor and then Associate Pastor of Trinity Lutheran Church in Moline, Illinois. As his hymnic avocation developed, he soon found some of his tunes, and indeed some of his texts as well, attracting attention from a variety of publishers. In the fall of 1991, Gloria Dei Lutheran Church in Rockford, Illinois extended a call to the 36-year-old Dr. Howard M. Edwards, III to become their Senior Pastor. As a result he, Lori, and their two children are now putting down roots in that community. I recount this pilgrimmage to convey some sense of the urgency and excitement that surrounds this young hymnwriter. In the business world we would say he is a "fast-tracking" hymnwriter which is surely an oxymoron if ever there was one. Fanny Crosby wrote her first hymn at age 44, and Fred Pratt Green penned his first effort at age 65. Nothing moves quickly in hymn publishing circles and the last Foreword I wrote introduced the hymns of J.R. Peacey in a book entitled **GO FORTH FOR GOD.** This was published in 1991, exactly twenty years after Peacey's death. So who is this young upstart, and how did he get there so quickly?

Rusty Edwards claims a proud heritage which reaches back to Martin Luther, the great reformer. Surely the Lutheran tradition of hymn singing and writing is a well-documented and cherished lineage. Each generation has produced its own paradigms of this developing art form adding a rich texture to the voice of God's people through congregational song.

The purpose of this collection is to introduce the talents of this new Lutheran voice to a wider audience. It will quickly become obvious that he is ecumenical in that he cares about and writes for the whole church—indeed, the whole world. Inclusive language is a given in Rusty Edwards' works. He did not have to go through a "transition stage" and he carries none of the linguistic baggage of the '60s and '70s. His knowledge of the Bible helps him articulate theology with clear and uncluttered directness. Literary grace permeates his original texts and his paraphrases are well focused. Fresh metaphors and picture language abound.

Musically, Rusty is a great admirer of Dave Brubeck and Chick Corea. His melodies are durable and singable, and his frequent use of jazz harmonies lends a contemporary flavor to his compositions. Rusty's gentleness shows up often in his work, especially in tunes like *Corea* and *Beth*. Although he writes tunes and texts equally well, he almost always chooses to share the hymn-creating process with another writer.

The "British Hymn Explosion" of the '80s has come and gone, as have many of its exponents. Who will fill the shoes of Albert Bayly, Erik Routley, Cyril Taylor, and John W. Wilson—just to name a few? Where will this new generation of hymnwriters be found? I suggest that the torch has already been passed and is burning brightly in Rockford, Illinois. We are excited about the opportunity to present this collection of works from an emerging, prolific representative of the new generation of hymnwriters. Rusty Edwards has arrived like a breath of fresh air, and I predict that the hymns in this collection will have wide use. The gift and the promise is there and I am also convinced that the best is yet to come. So the publishers of church music in the 21st century need not despair; indeed, they will have a great deal to look forward to.

George H. Shorney, Chairman
HOPE PUBLISHING COMPANY
Labor Day, 1992

ACKNOWLEDGEMENTS

My sincere thanks:

To God, for loving unconditionally, and for allowing me the privilege of sharing news of faith, hope, and love through song.

To Lori, Benjamin, and Ian for love, joy, laughter, and for the many sacrifices you have made for me. I love you deeply and cherish your love.

To my parents for not stopping at three children and for raising me gracefully.

To Coggin, Susan, and Mary, my sisters.

To all who have given my life nourishment and direction.

To Eileen Gulley and Tom and Clare Anderson, for grace.

To Braden Canfield and Peter and Cheri Duys, for listening.

To The Hymn Society, for affirmation and support.

To Chick Corea for being the most profound musical influence in my life, and for writing the Foreword.

To Dave Brubeck, for awakening my rhythmic pulse.

To David Nott and Dale Ganz for giving me an interest in sacred music.

To Gracia Grindal and Jaroslav Vajda for teaching me text writing.

To Carl Schalk and Steve Steely for teaching me hymn composition/arranging.

To Herb Brokering, Nancy Malone, and Robley Whitson, creative ministry teachers.

To the people of Trinity/Moline and Gloria Dei/Rockford congregations.

To Bob Blew for the Door County photo.

To each of this book's contributors for blessing my work with theirs.

To Jack Schrader, Doris and Bill Wagner, and all my friends at Hope Publishing Company for taking such loving care with the material and for making this collection available.

To George Shorney, for guidance, patience, creative freedom, and for writing the Introduction.

To all who sing these songs. Be blessed! Be free!

Rusty Edwards

1   As the Moon Is to the Sun

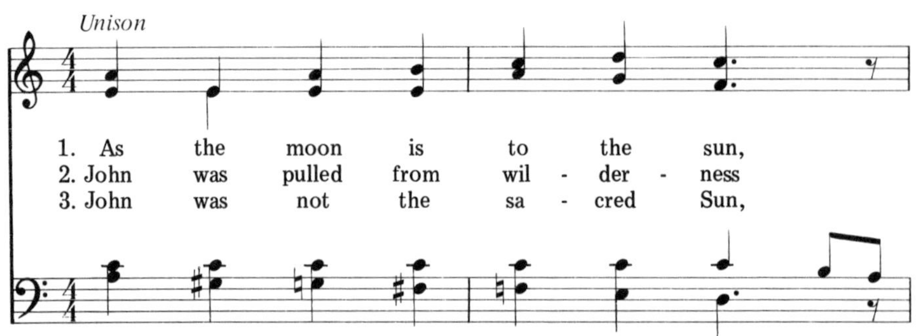

Unison
1. As the moon is to the sun,
2. John was pulled from wil - der - ness
3. John was not the sa - cred Sun,

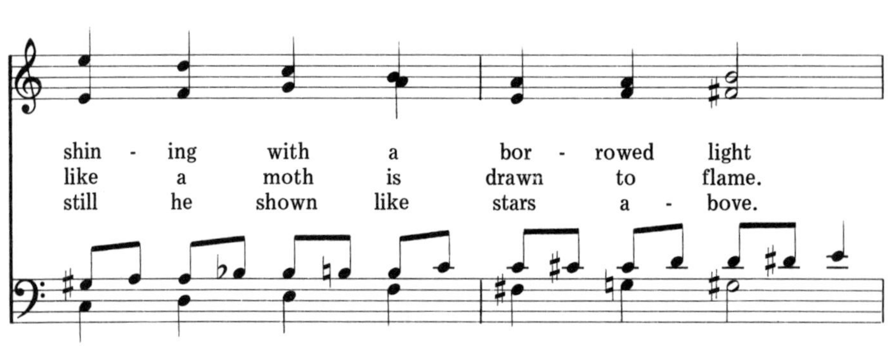

shin - ing with a bor - rowed light
like a moth is drawn to flame.
still he shown like stars a - bove.

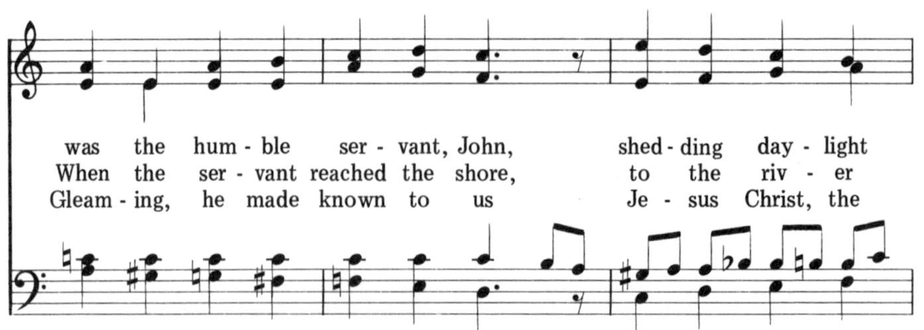

was the hum - ble ser - vant, John, shed - ding day - light
When the ser - vant reached the shore, to the riv - er
Gleam - ing, he made known to us Je - sus Christ, the

WORDS: Rusty Edwards
MUSIC: Dave Brubeck

BORROWED LIGHT
7.7.7.7.D.

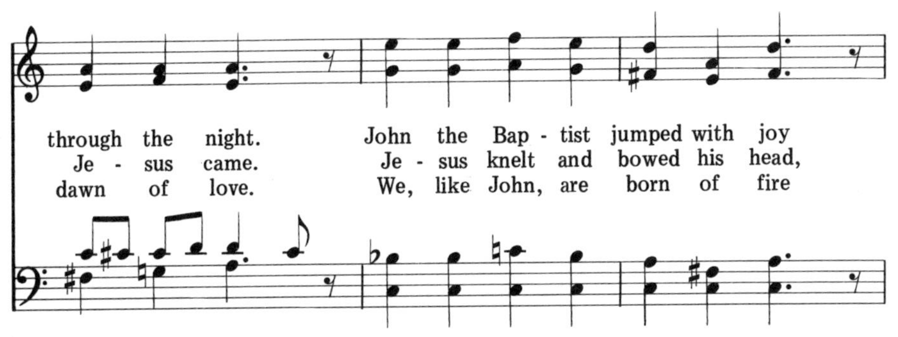

through the night.   John the Bap - tist jumped with joy
Je - sus came.   Je - sus knelt and bowed his head,
dawn of love.   We, like John, are born of fire

long be - fore his na - tal day.   He was not to
asked the ser - vant to bap - tize.   John would smile as
e - ven in this world to - day.   May our God shine

be the Christ,   but he came to point the way.
heav - en said,   "Let my Star of Day a - rise!"
light on us   that we may give love a - way.

2 Behold, a Woman from the City

Unison

1. Be - hold, a wom-an from the cit - y came to the
2. Be - hold, the wom-an kissed and washed him, dry - ing him
3. Then he re - buked the pi - ous Si - mon, "Tell me, my
4. "Be - hold, the wom-an is re - pen - tant. See how she

place where Je - sus ate, brought a box of pre - cious
with her love - ly hair, shock-ing those who sat with
friend, who would love more, one who had been much for -
gives her fin - est oil, for she has been much for -

oint - ment with her tears the wom - an washed his
Je - sus e - ven though they saw the wom - an's
giv - en or the one whose sins were small and
giv - en." Then he said un - to the wom - an,

feet, weep - ing as the Sav - ior ate.
tears, "Does not Je - sus know of her?"
few? Who would weep the bit - t'rest tear?
"Go, go your faith has made you whole."

WORDS: Gracia Grindal
MUSIC: Rusty Edwards

TEARS
9.8.8.9.7.

Brother Sun, Sister Moon

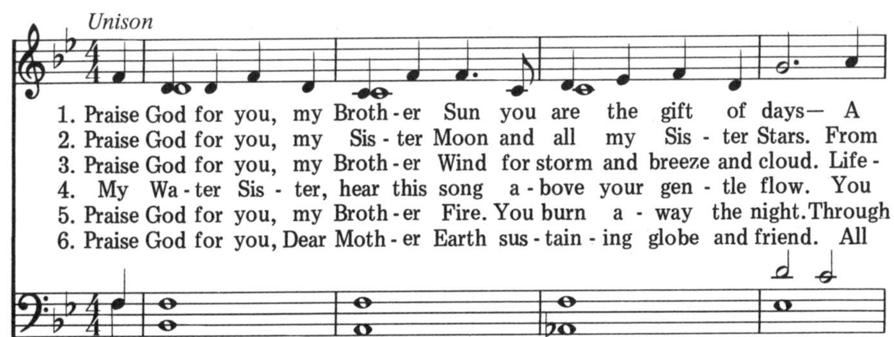
Unison
1. Praise God for you, my Broth-er Sun you are the gift of days— A
2. Praise God for you, my Sis-ter Moon and all my Sis-ter Stars. From
3. Praise God for you, my Broth-er Wind for storm and breeze and cloud. Life-
4. My Wa-ter Sis-ter, hear this song a-bove your gen-tle flow. You
5. Praise God for you, my Broth-er Fire. You burn a-way the night. Through
6. Praise God for you, Dear Moth-er Earth sus-tain-ing globe and friend. All

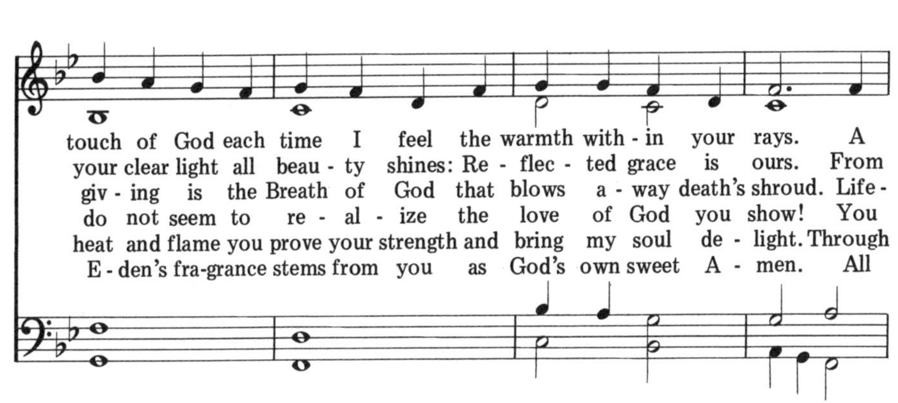
touch of God each time I feel the warmth with-in your rays. A
your clear light all beau-ty shines: Re-flec-ted grace is ours. From
giv-ing is the Breath of God that blows a-way death's shroud. Life-
do not seem to re-al-ize the love of God you show! You
heat and flame you prove your strength and bring my soul de-light. Through
E-den's fra-grance stems from you as God's own sweet A-men. All

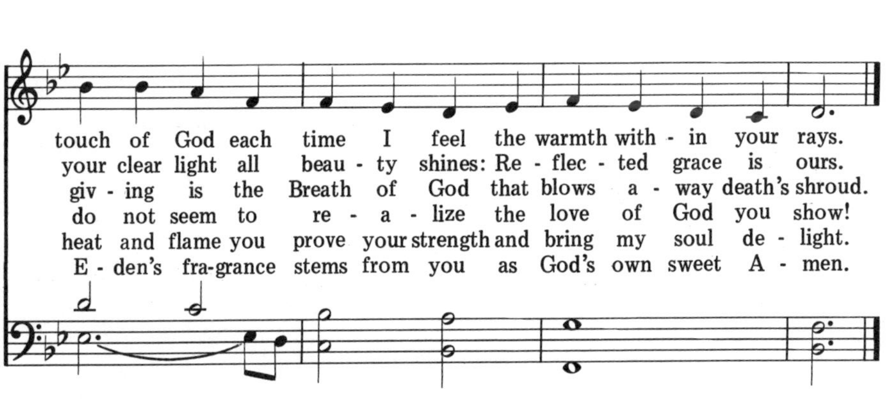
touch of God each time I feel the warmth with-in your rays.
your clear light all beau-ty shines: Re-flec-ted grace is ours.
giv-ing is the Breath of God that blows a-way death's shroud.
do not seem to re-a-lize the love of God you show!
heat and flame you prove your strength and bring my soul de-light.
E-den's fra-grance stems from you as God's own sweet A-men.

WORDS: St. Francis of Assisi; versification Rusty Edwards
MUSIC: Rusty Edwards

COREA
8.6.8.6.8.6.

4 Come, Little Children

Unison
1. Come, lit - tle chil - dren, to the si - lent man - ger.
2. Come, lit - tle chil - dren, to the lit - tle bro - ther.
3. Come, lit - tle chil - dren, to the God of glo - ry.
Come, lit - tle chil - dren, see the mys - ter - y.
Come, lit - tle chil - dren, hear the ba - by cry.
Come, lit - tle chil - dren, see the Light of light.
Come, lit - tle chil - dren, to the lit - tle stran - ger.
Come, lit - tle chil - dren, see the Ma - ry moth - er.
Come, lit - tle chil - dren, hear the gos - pel sto - ry.
Come, lit - tle chil - dren, to na - tiv - i - ty.
Come, lit - tle chil - dren, see the star on high.
Come, lit - tle chil - dren, it is Christ - mas night.

WORDS: Herbert F. Brokering
MUSIC: Rusty Edwards, arr. Robert Sterling

HOWARD
11.10.11.10.

Faith Is the Yes of the Heart

Unison
1. Faith is the yes of the heart and the
2. Faith is the blush of the mind and the
3. Faith sees the Christ in the bread and the
4. Faith feels the day be-fore dawn, smells the
5. Faith is a rain - bow in rain and a

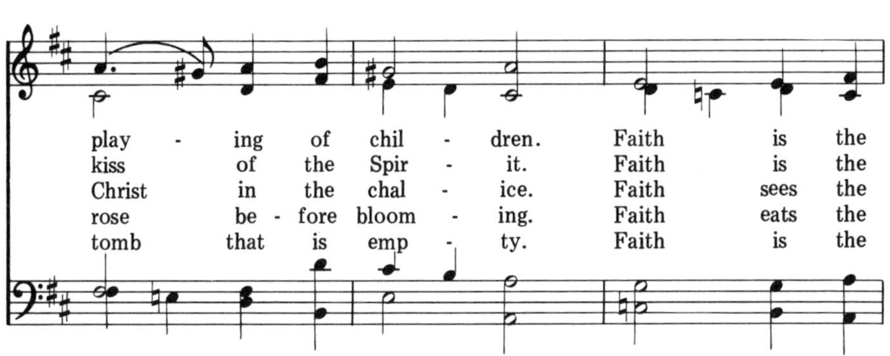

play - ing of chil - dren. Faith is the
kiss of the Spir - it. Faith is the
Christ in the chal - ice. Faith sees the
rose be - fore bloom - ing. Faith eats the
tomb that is emp - ty. Faith is the

walk in the dark and the ring for the wed - ding.
moth - er of love and the child in the mak - ing.
rise from the dead and the shar - ing of har - vest.
heav - en - ly feast, hears the sound of God's trum - pet.
end from the start and be - gin - nings in end - ings.

WORDS: Rusty Edwards
MUSIC: Jane Marshall

ROCKFORD
7.7.7.7.

6   For God So Loved the World

Refrain
Unison
For God so loved the world that God gave the on-ly Son,
Fine
that who-ev-er be-lieves in him shall have e-ter-nal life.
1. As Mo-ses lift-ed the ser-pent in the wil-der-ness,
2. For God sent Je-sus from heav-en to this world of ours
3. For sure-ly Je-sus would tell us that we must be born
D.C. al Fine
so the Son of God must be lift-ed that we may have life.
not to curse the world but to save us that we may have life.
of the wa-ter and of the spir-it that we may have life.

WORDS and MUSIC: Rusty Edwards

THREE SIXTEEN
8.5.9.5.Ref.

Give Thanks to God on High

Unison

1. Give thanks to God on high for saints of oth-er days, whose
2. Their vi-sion long-ful-filled, our prayer is still the same: up-
3. New tasks to-day are ours who serve a world in pain, new
4. Give thanks to God on high for all the fu-ture sends, in

hope it was to live and die in love's con-sum-ing blaze, for
on their work of faith to build, their word of truth pro-claim, for
calls to chal-lenge all our powers of heart and hand and brain, for
praise of Christ to live and die who calls his ser-vants friends, for

Christ and his king-dom, for Christ and his king-dom, for
Christ and his king-dom, for Christ and his king-dom, for
Christ and his king-dom, for Christ and his king-dom, for
Christ and his king-dom, for Christ and his king-dom, for

Christ and his king-dom, his glo-ry and his praise.
Christ and his king-dom, and for his ho-ly name.
Christ and his king-dom, while life and breath re-main.
Christ and his king-dom, whose glo-ry nev-er ends!

WORDS: Timothy Dudley-Smith
MUSIC: Rusty Edwards

LUDY
6.6.8.6.6.6.6.6.

8 God, We Praise You!

1. God, we praise you! God, we bless you! God, we name you sov-ereign Lord!
2. True a - pos - tles, faith - ful proph - ets, saints who set their world a - blaze,
3. Je - sus Christ, the king of glo - ry, ev - er - last - ing Son of God,
4. Christ, at God's right hand vic - to - rious, you will judge the world you made;

Might - y King whom an - gels wor - ship, Fa - ther, by your church a - dored:
mar - tyrs, once un-known, un - heed - ed, join one grow-ing song of praise,
hum - ble was your vir - gin moth - er, hard the lone - ly path you trod:
Lord, in mer - cy help your ser - vants for whose free-dom you have paid:

all cre - a - tion shows your glo - ry, heaven and earth draw near your throne
while your church on earth con-fess-es one ma - jes - tic Trin - i - ty:
by your cross is sin de - feat - ed, hell con-front - ed face to face,
raise us up from dust to glo - ry, guard us from all sin to - day;

sing - ing "Ho - ly, ho - ly, ho - ly, Lord of hosts, and God a - lone!"
Fa - ther, Son, and Ho - ly Spir - it, God, our hope e - ter - nal - ly.
heav - en o - pened to be - liev - ers, sin - ners jus - ti - fied by grace.
King en-throned a - bove all prais - es, save your peo - ple, God, we pray.

WORDS: Christopher Idle; para. of *Te Deum laudamus*
MUSIC: Rusty Edwards

ILA
8.7.8.7.D.

How Lovely Is Thy Dwelling Place   9

Unison

1. How love - ly is thy dwell - ing place, O
2. Be - side thine al - tars, gra - cious Lord, the
3. They who go through the des - ert vale will
4. One day with - in thy courts ex - cels a

Lord of Hosts, to me! My thir - sty soul de -
swal - lows find a nest; how hap - py they who
find it filled with springs, and they shall climb from
thou - sand spent a - way; how hap - py they who

sires and longs with - in thy courts to be; my
dwell with thee and praise thee with - out rest, and
height to height till Zi - on's tem - ple rings with
keep thy laws nor from thy pre - cepts stray, for

ver - y heart and flesh cry out, O liv - ing God, for thee.
hap - py they whose hearts are set up - on the pil - grim's quest.
praise to thee, in glo - ry throned, Lord God, great King of kings.
thou shalt sure - ly bless all those who live the words they pray.

WORDS: St. 1 and 2, The Psalms of David in *Meter*, 1650; St. 3 and 4, Carl P. Daw, Jr.
MUSIC: Rusty Edwards

COREA
8.6.8.6.8.6.

10   I Hear Creation Groaning

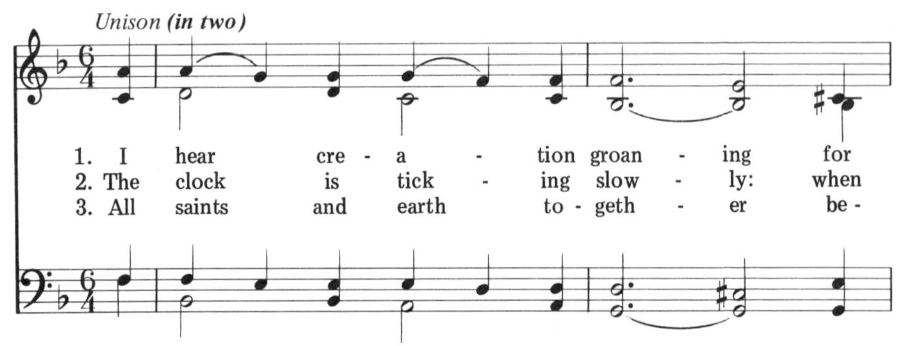

Unison (in two)
1. I hear cre - a - tion groan - ing for
2. The clock is tick - ing slow - ly: when
3. All saints and earth to - geth - er be -

what it can - not see; a cry of an - cient
will this fu - ture live? We, too, ache for to -
gin the na - tal song. A world is in the

long - ing for dreams to be set
mor - row and pray for some re -
mak - ing where you and I be -

WORDS: Rusty Edwards
MUSIC: Jane Marshall

FRIEDMAN
7.6.7.6.D.

free. How long by pa - tient wait - ing can
lief. Sharp pangs re - mind of prom - ise as
long. The urge keeps grow - ing strong - er: the

na - ture bear the pain of la - bor cul - mi -
if to let us know the hour of God is
birth - ing has be - gun. Our fo - cus will sus -

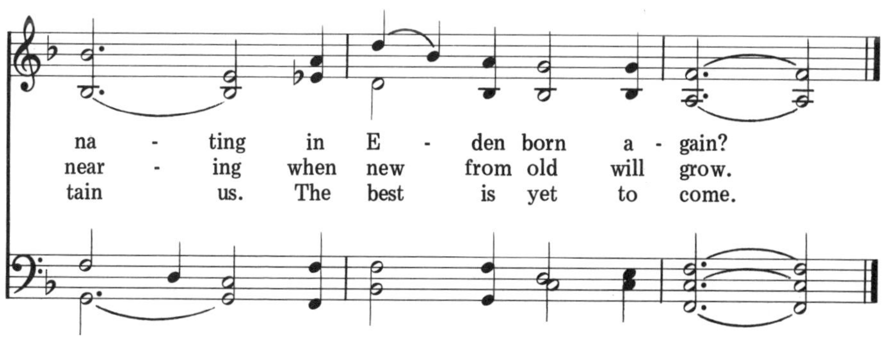

na - ting in E - den born a - gain?
near - ing when new from old will grow.
tain us. The best is yet to come.

I Will Not Forget You

Refrain (not too fast)
Unison
I will not for-get you. I will not for-get.
You are al-ways in my mem-o-ry. I will not for-get.
Fine
1. You may say that I have for-sak-en you. You may
2. Can a moth-er for-get her new-born child? Can she
3. Though I love you and will re-mem-ber you, you still
say you are all a-lone and I seem far a-way. But I
have no com-pas-sion on her daugh-ter or her son? E-ven
ask how I keep you in my heart and on my mind. You are

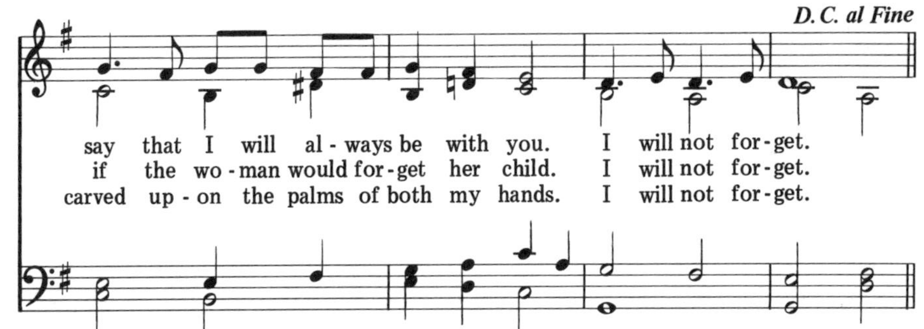

D.C. al Fine
say that I will al-ways be with you.   I will not for-get.
if the wo-man would for-get her child.   I will not for-get.
carved up-on the palms of both my hands.   I will not for-get.

In Jesus' Name, We Pause to Pray   12
(A New Table Prayer)

In Je - sus' Name we pause to pray: give
us our dai - ly bread to - day, bless us with strength, that
we may bless our neigh - bor out of grate - ful - ness.

WORDS: Rusty Edwards
MUSIC: Thomas Tallis

TALLIS CANON
L.M.

13 In the Dark of Easter Morning

Unison

1. In the dark of Eas - ter morn - ing Ma - ry Mag - da - lene did stand
2. When they saw the lin - en wrap - ping John and Si - mon did be - lieve.
3. Je - sus stood by weep - ing Ma - ry, "Whom, my la - dy, do you seek?"
4. "I must go un - to my Fa - ther, to your Fa - ther and our God.

by the grave of Je - sus mourn - ing for the death of Christ her friend;
Both dis - ci - ples left her weep - ing, weep - ing there out - side the grave.
"Sir, if you have found his bo - dy, tell me, please, for his dear sake."
Tell the oth - ers I am com - ing and that you have seen the Lord."

then she saw the gap - ing en - trance where the stone was rolled a - way;
Peer - ing in she saw two an - gels. "Why, my la - dy do you weep?"
Je - sus said un - to her, "Ma - ry." Ma - ry turned and saw her friend.
Ma - ry went to the dis - ci - ples full of won - der, love, and praise,

quick she ran to John and Pe - ter, cry - ing, "Broth - ers, come and see!"
"They have ta - ken Je - sus' bo - dy whom my spic - es were to keep."
"Lord," she cried and reached to touch him, "touch me not till I as - cend."
wait - ing for him in the bod - y, ris - en mir - a - cle of grace.

Lamp of God Unveiled

1. Lamp of God un-veiled in the star-ry night.
2. Light un-veiled a-gain at the riv-er's edge.
3. Strength of God un-veiled; wa-ter turned to wine.
4. Word un-veiled once more high up-on a hill.

Wis-dom from the east knelt be-fore the sight.
As the heir was cleansed and re-ceived Love's pledge.
Wed-ding guests trans-formed hav-ing seen di-vine.
Hear good news re-vealed: Je-sus is God's Will.

Plan of God ex-posed through e-piph-a-ny.

Shine on, mid-night star! Give us light to see.

WORDS: Rusty Edwards
MUSIC: Hu Te-ai; arr. Bliss Wiant

LE P'ING
5.5.5.5.D.

15 Lift Your Voice Rejoicing, Mary

Unison

1. Lift your voice re-joic-ing, Ma - ry, Christ is ris - en from the
2. Raise your wear - y eye-lids, Ma - ry, see him liv - ing ev - er-
3. Life is yours for-ev - er, Ma - ry, for your light is come once

tomb: on the cross a suf-fering vic - tim, now as vic - tor he is
more; see his coun - te-nance how gra-cious; see the wounds for you he
more; and the strength of death is bro - ken; now your songs of joy out-

come. Whom your tears in death were mourn - ing, wel - come
bore. All the glo - ry of the morn - ing pales be-
pour. End - ed now the night of sor - row; love has

with your smiles re - turn - ing. Let your al - le - lu - ias rise!
fore those wounds re - deem - ing. Let your al - le - lu - ias rise!
brought the bless - ed mor - row. Let your al - le - lu - ias rise!

WORDS: Latin, tr. Elizabeth Rundle Charles
MUSIC: Rusty Edwards

TALITHA CUMI
8.7.8.7.8.8.7.

Lord of Feasting and of Hunger 16

Unison
1. Lord of feast - ing and of hun - ger, give us
2. Lord of seed and Lord of har - vest, turn the
3. Lord of storm and heat and dan - ger, deep in -
4. Lord of tak - ing and of giv - ing, give us
eyes to see your bread in the mir - a - cle of
des - ert in - to bloom; pur - i - fy the sky and
side and high a - bove, break in - to all fear and
back our dig - ni - ty; in our u - ni - ver - sal
won - der, till all ta - bles will be fed.
for - est, give your wis - dom; send it soon.
an - ger, till you reign the earth in love.
liv - ing, break down all in - eq - ui - ty.
Refrain
See the si - lent ones who wait when the bless-ing seems too late.

WORDS: Herbert F. Brokering
MUSIC: Rusty Edwards; arr. Carl Schalk

CRONMILLER
8.7.8.7.Ref.

17 Lord of the Living

Unison

1. Lord of the liv - ing, in your name as -
2. Help us to trea - sure all that will re -
3. May we, when - ev - er tempt - ed to de -
4. Lord, you can lift us from the grave of

sem - bled, we join to thank you for the life re -
mind us of the en - rich - ment in the days be -
jec - tion, strong - ly re - cap - ture thoughts of res - ur -
sor - row in - to the pres - ence of your own to -

mem - bered. Fa - ther have mer - cy, to your chil - dren
hind us. Your love has set us in the gen - er -
rec - tion. You gave us Je - sus to de - feat our
mor - row; give to your peo - ple for the day's af -

giv - ing hope in be - liev - ing.
a - tions, God of cre - a - tion.
sad - ness with Eas - ter glad - ness.
flic - tion your ben - e - dic - tion.

WORDS: Fred Kaan
MUSIC: Rusty Edwards

FORT WORTH
11.11.11.5.

Loving Spirit

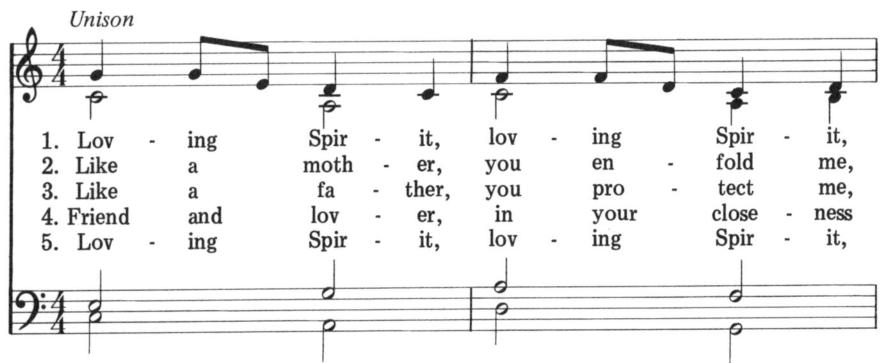

Unison
1. Lov - ing   Spir - it, lov - ing   Spir - it,
2. Like   a   moth - er,   you   en - fold   me,
3. Like   a   fa - ther,   you   pro - tect   me,
4. Friend   and   lov - er,   in   your   close - ness
5. Lov - ing   Spir - it,   lov - ing   Spir - it,

you   have cho - sen   me   to   be—   you   have drawn   me
hold   my   life with - in   your own,   feed   me   with your
teach   me   the   dis - cern - ing   eye,   hoist   me   up   up -
I   am known and   held   and blessed: in   your prom - ise
you   have cho - sen   me   to   be—   you   have drawn   me

to   your won - der,   you   have   set   your sign   on   me.
ver - y   bod - y,   form   me   of   your flesh   and   bone.
on   your shoul - der,   let   me   see   the   world from   high.
is   my   com - fort,   in   your pres - ence   I   may   rest.
to   your won - der,   you   have   set   your sign   on   me.

WORDS: Shirley Erena Murray
MUSIC: Rusty Edwards

BETH
8.7.8.7.

19 New Days Are Coming

Unison
1. New days are com - ing, Christ is ar - riv - ing,
2. Life in the new earth will be de - light - ful:
3. El - ders and chil - dren share the a - bun - dance:
4. In ex - pec - ta - tion of the ar - riv - al,
old life for - got - ten, new life is near!
there will be plen - ty for all to eat.
no more shall work - ers la - bor in vain.
an - tic - i - pa - tion fills us with joy!
God will trans - form us, and earth a - round us.
Li - ons and ox - en din - ing to - geth - er
All will have ac - cess to the Cre - a - tor;
So let us wor - ship in truth and glad - ness,
There will be laugh - ter, no long - er tears!
shall be the sign of Sa - tan's de - feat.
mer - cy and jus - tice pour - ing like rain.
that high - est prais - es God may en - joy!

WORDS and MUSIC: Rusty Edwards

ANN'S ORDINATION
5.5.5.4.D.

Now It Is Evening

Unison
1. Now it is eve - ning lights of the cit - y
2. Now it is eve - ning food on the ta - ble
3. Now it is eve - ning lit - tle ones sleep - ing
4. Now it is eve - ning here in our meet - ing
Ped.
bid us re - mem - ber Christ is our Light.
bids us re - mem - ber Christ is our Life.
bid us re - mem - ber Christ is our peace.
may we re - mem - ber Christ is our Friend.
Man - y are lone - ly, who will be neigh - bor?
Man - y are hun - gry, who will be neigh - bor?
Some are ne - glect - ed, who will be neigh - bor?
Some may be strang - ers who will be neigh - bor?
Where there is car - ing Christ is our Light.
Where there is shar - ing Christ is our Life.
Where there is car - ing Christ is our peace.
Where there's a wel - come Christ is our friend.

WORDS: Fred Pratt Green
MUSIC: Rusty Edwards

BOZEMAN
5.5.5.4.D.

Nothing in This World

Noth - ing in this world can shake you,
cut you off, or sep - a - rate you from the love of
God in Je - sus. Moun-tain height nor o - cean deep - ness.
1. Not our laugh - ter or our cry - ing, not our fi - nal
2. Not the pres - ent, nor the fu - ture, not a grand or
3. Not the clutch - ing hand of dan - ger, not our sad - ness
4. Not the lure of an - y na - tion, noth - ing else in

WORDS: Rusty Edwards
MUSIC: Dave Brubeck

AGAPETOS
8.8.8.8.8.8.8.9.9.10.8.Coda

hour of dy - ing. Love from God is not oc - ca - sion - al.
wick - ed crea - ture. Love from God is not oc - ca - sion - al.
or our an - ger. Love from God is not oc - ca - sion - al.
all cre - a - tion. Love from God is not oc - ca - sion - al.

Love from God is un - con - di - tion - al. Hear this ech - o in -

D.C.

to e - ter - ni - ty: Je - sus loves you. Je - sus loves you.
After Verse 4, go to Coda.

Coda

There is one prom-ise you can re - ly on: Je - sus Christ will al - ways love you.

22 Now Let Us from This Table Rise

1. Now let us from this ta - ble rise, re -
2. With minds a - lert, up - held by grace, to
3. To fill each hu - man house with love, it
4. Then grant us cour - age, Fa - ther - God, to

newed in bod - y, mind and soul: with
spread the word in speech and deed, we
is the sac - ra - ment of care; the
choose a - gain the pil - grim way; and

Christ we die and live a - gain, his
fol - low in the steps of Christ, at
work that Christ be - gan to do we
help us to ac - cept with joy the

self - less love has made us whole.
one with all in hope and need.
hum - bly pledge our - selves to share.
chal - lenge of to - mor - row's day.

WORDS: Fred Kaan
MUSIC: Rusty Edwards

LORRAINE
L.M.

Praise the One

23

Unison
1. Praise the One who breaks the dark-ness with a lib - er - at - ing light.
2. Praise the One who blessed the chil-dren with a strong yet gen - tle word.
3. Praise the one true love in - car-nate: Christ who suf-fered in our place.
Praise the One who frees the pris-oners turn-ing blind-ness in - to sight.
Praise the One who drove out de-mons with a pierc-ing two - edged sword.
Je - sus died and rose for man - y that we may know God by grace.
Praise the One who preached the Gos-pel heal - ing ev - ery dread dis-ease.
Praise the One who brings cool wa - ter to the des - ert's burn-ing sand.
Let us sing for joy and glad-ness see - ing what our God has done.
Calm - ing storms and feed - ing thou-sands with the ver - y bread of peace.
From this well comes liv - ing wat - er quench-ing thirst in ev - ery land.
Praise the one re - deem-ing glo - ry. Praise the One who makes us one.

WORDS: Rusty Edwards
MUSIC: Paul Manz

HULDA
8.7.8.7.D.

24 Princes, Paupers, Royal Children

Unison

1. Prin - ces, pau - pers, roy - al chil-dren all in need of God's em - brace;
2. O - pen wide your an - cient vis - tas, 'til on tip - toe we will see
3. Turn my heart to see the oth - er not as strang-er or as foe
4. Con - se-crate our fields and foun-tains; pur - i - fy our sun and rain
5. One the way for all the plead-ing one the truth for all the lies.

saints and an - gels feast on mer - cy, earth and heav - en feast on grace.
love that on - ly makes the dif-f'rence: love the glimpse of u - ni - ty.
make our neigh-bor, sis - ter, broth - er, for the miles and years to go.
ded - i - cate our ho - ly ta - ble 'til cre - a - tion sings a - gain.
One the life for all suc-ceed - ing one the rain-bow of the skies.

One com - pas-sion, one de - vo - tion, one the love of all who love.
One the dream-ers, one e - mo - tion, one the Spir - it, one the bond,
Give the joy of vol - un - teer-ing so we feel the love of grace;
One the sis - ter, one the broth-er; one the hu - man fam - i - ly.
One the prom-ise, one the tend-ing one the love there is to be.

We the beg-gars of God's wel-fare: love in touch with love a - bove.
one the want-ing, one the beg-ging, one the pres - ent, one be - yond.
in the won-der-ment of ser - vice. Bring cre - a - tion face to face.
One the life with one an - oth - er; one God's end-less char - i - ty.
One the dreams of hope un - end-ing one, all one, e - ter - nal - ly.

WORDS: Herbert F. Brokering
MUSIC: Rusty Edwards

ROCK ISLAND
8.7.8.7.D.

Rejoice and Prepare Now

Brightly (♩ = 100)

1. Re - joice and pre - pare now the way of the Lord.
2. Re - joice and pre - pare for a mir - a - cle birth.
3. Re - joice and pre - pare for our God is at hand.
4. Re - joice and pre - pare for God's pow - er is near.

Make read - y a path for the life - sav - ing Word.
Pre - pare for a gift of re - mark - a - ble worth.
Ring bells and sound trum - pets all o - ver this land.
And short - ly the glo - ry of God will ap - pear.

Make straight in the des - ert a suit - a - ble road
Lift up ev - ery val - ley; the moun - tains make low
Come, gath - er to - geth - er to wel - come this Guest.
This light in the dark - ness will show us the way.

that all flesh shall see the sal - va - tion of God.
so all of the earth may be - lieve, see, and know.
Pre - pare to sing prais - es; pre - pare to be blest.
Re - joice and pre - pare for this great hol - i - day.

WORDS: Rusty Edwards
MUSIC: Ronald Watson

RESTORATION
11.11.11.11.

Small Things Count

Unison
1. Small things count, so Je - sus said—
2. Small things make the big things grow—
3. Ev - ery hair that's on our head,
cups of wa - ter, crumbs of bread,
yeast that bub - bles in the dough,
ev - ery spar - row, Je - sus said,
small things done be - cause we're kind count as big things
puffs that fill a big bal - loon, notes that make a
God takes care of, counts and knows— God loves us from
1,2
3
in God's mind.
hap - py tune.
top to toes!

WORDS: Shirley Erena Murray

MUSIC: Rusty Edwards

BENJAMIN'S SWING

7.7.7.7.

The Desert Shall Rejoice

Unison

The des - ert shall re - joice and blos - som as a rose,

1. it shall blos - som a - bun - dant-
2. for the ears of the deaf shall
3. for the tongue of the mute shall
4. for the ground will be - come a
5. as the ran - somed re - turn to
6. un - to Zi - on we come with

ly and re - joice with praise and sing - ing.
hear and the blind, their eyes be o - pened.
sing and the lame will dance with glad - ness.
pool and the dry land springs of wa - ter.
God and come sing - ing back to Zi - on.
joy for our God has come to save us.

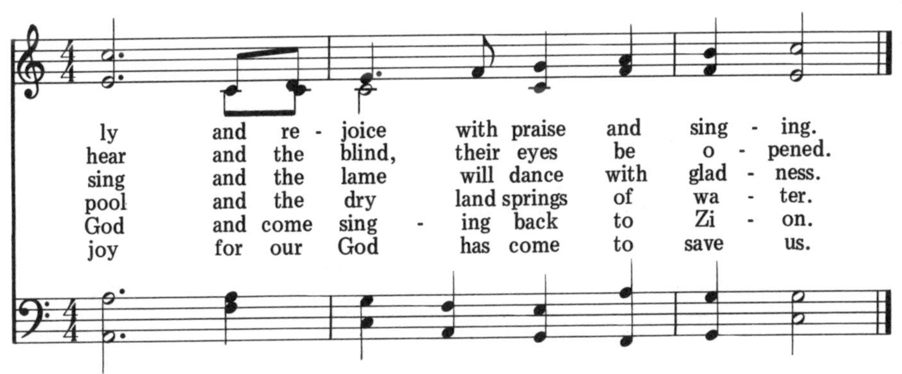

WORDS: Gracia Grindal
MUSIC: Rusty Edwards

ADVENT ROSE
6.6.8.8.

28 The Greatest Love of All

Unison

1. The great - est love of all is
2. The great - est love is God who
3. The strength that will not fail is
4. What is the length of love? How

love that nev - er ends; Great - er than an - y ro -
lis - tens through your fear. Nev - er a - gain will you
ev - er on God's mind. Love hopes be - yond all our
far will this love go? Love gives up life for a

mance or love be - tween two friends.
shed an un - im - por - tant tear.
dreams. The eyes of God are kind.
friend or ev - en for a foe.

Refrain

May your heart be filled with the great - est love of all.

WORDS and MUSIC: Rusty Edwards

VALENTINE
6.6.7.6.Ref.

To a Maid Engaged to Joseph   29

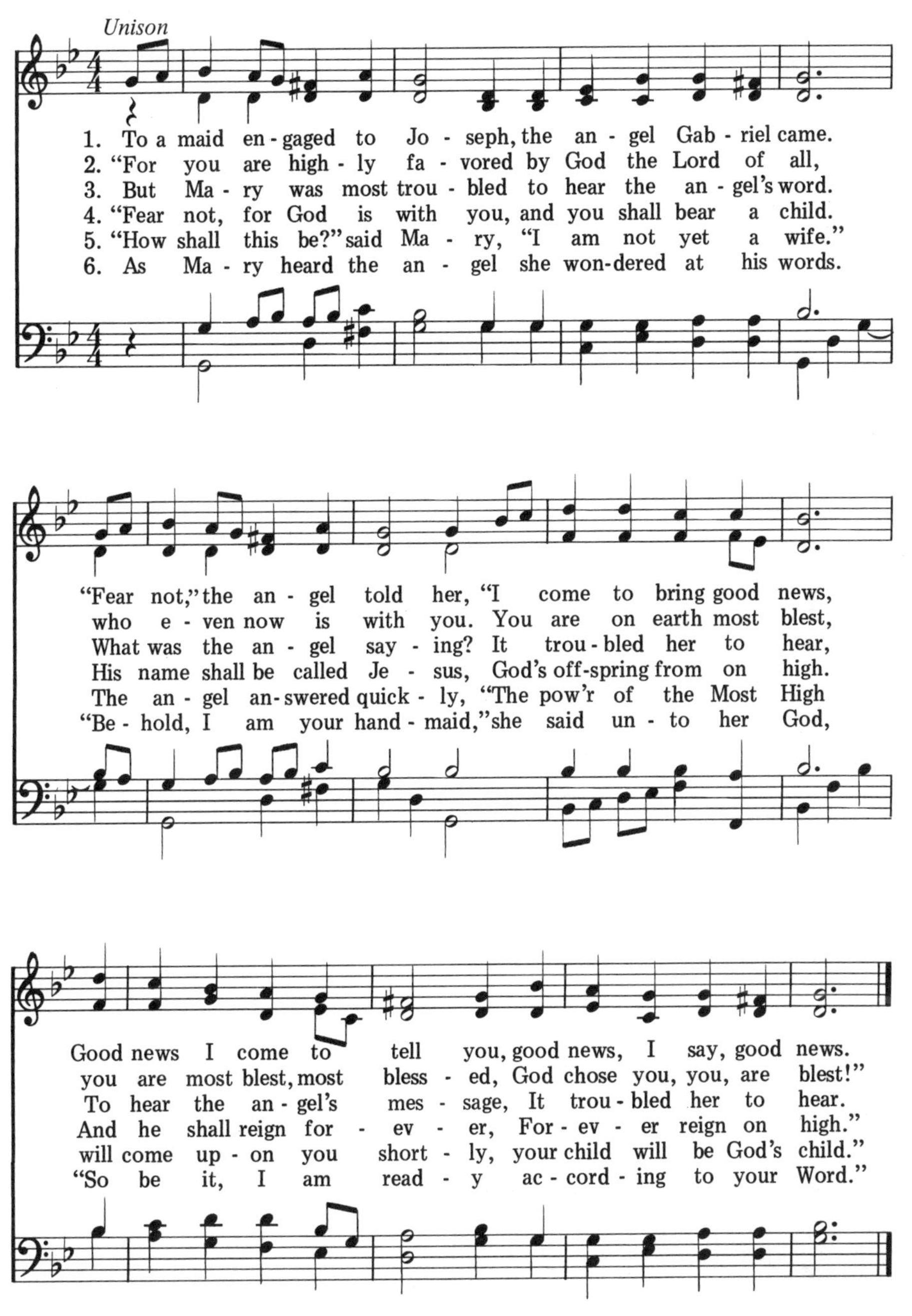

Unison
1. To a maid en-gaged to Jo-seph, the an-gel Gab-riel came.
2. "For you are high-ly fa-vored by God the Lord of all,
3. But Ma-ry was most trou-bled to hear the an-gel's word.
4. "Fear not, for God is with you, and you shall bear a child.
5. "How shall this be?" said Ma-ry, "I am not yet a wife."
6. As Ma-ry heard the an-gel she won-dered at his words.

"Fear not," the an-gel told her, "I come to bring good news,
who e-ven now is with you. You are on earth most blest,
What was the an-gel say-ing? It trou-bled her to hear,
His name shall be called Je-sus, God's off-spring from on high.
The an-gel an-swered quick-ly, "The pow'r of the Most High
"Be-hold, I am your hand-maid," she said un-to her God,

Good news I come to tell you, good news, I say, good news.
you are most blest, most bless-ed, God chose you, you, are blest!"
To hear the an-gel's mes-sage, It trou-bled her to hear.
And he shall reign for-ev-er, For-ev-er reign on high."
will come up-on you short-ly, your child will be God's child."
"So be it, I am read-y ac-cord-ing to your Word."

WORDS: Gracia Grindal

MUSIC: Rusty Edwards

ANNUNCIATION
7.6.7.6.7.6.

Two People

1. Two peo - ple in the name of Christ are
2. We gath - er in the name of Christ to

now to - geth - er join - ing. Two
wit - ness this oc - ca - sion. We

lives be - come one fam - i - ly when
pray they put their trust in God who

they re - ceive God's bless - ing. Com -
gave them their sal - va - tion. May

WORDS: Rusty Edwards
MUSIC: Melody Johann Schop, alt.; harm. Johann Sebastian Bach

ERMUNTRE DICH
8.7.8.7.8.8.7.7.

mit - ted lives new steps now take as
two lives love, for rich, for poor and

sol - emn vows they soon will make. Faith,
know God loves them ev - en more. Faith,

hope, and love sur - round them. The
hope, and love sur - round them. The

grace of God has found them.
grace of God has found them.

We All Are One in Mission

Unison
1. We all are one in mis - sion, We
2. We all are called for ser - vice To
3. We all be - hold one vi - sion, A
4. Now let us be u - nit - ed And
Ped.

all are one in call, Our
wit - ness in God's name. Our
stark re - al - i - ty: The
let our song be heard. Now

var - ied gifts u - nit - ed By Christ, the Lord of
min - is - tries are dif - f'rent, Our pur - pose is the
stew - ard of sal - va - tion Was nailed up - on a
let us be a ves - sel For God's re - deem - ing

WORDS: Rusty Edwards
MUSIC: Dale Wood

ACCORD
7.6.7.6.D.

all. A sin - gle, great com - mis - sion Com -
same: To touch the lives of oth - ers By
tree. Yet res - ur - rect - ed Jus - tice Gives
Word. We all are one in mis - sion, We

pels us from a - bove To plan and work to -
God's sur - pris - ing grace So ev - 'ry folk and
rise that we may share Free re - con - cil - i -
all are one in call, Our var - ied gifts u -

geth - er That all may know Christ's love.
na - tion May feel God's warm em - brace.
a - tion And hope a - mid de - spair.
nit - ed By Christ, the Lord of all.

We Bow Before You, God

32

Unison
1. We bow be - fore you, God, our
2. We bow be - fore you, God, our
3. We bow be - fore you, God, our

source and rich - est plea - sure. We pray that God will
source and rich - est plea - sure. For Christ has come to
source and rich - est plea - sure. O Christ, work truth and

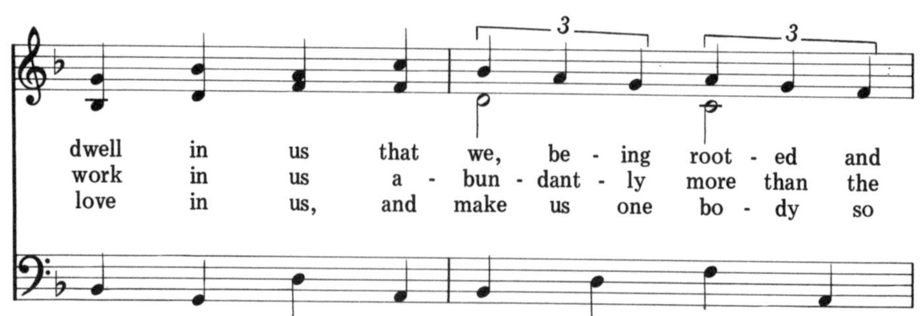

dwell in us that we, be - ing root - ed and
work in us a - bun - dant - ly more than the
love in us, and make us one bo - dy so

WORDS: Gracia Grindal
MUSIC: Rusty Edwards

EPHESIAN
6.7.8.11.8.7.6.7.

ground - ed in love may have pow - er to com - pre -
most we could ask, he has come to make all things
we may be whole, knit to - geth - er in ev' - ry

hend Christ's love which has no mea - sure. We
new, O Christ, our pur - est trea - sure. We
part, em - pow'red to do your plea - sure. We

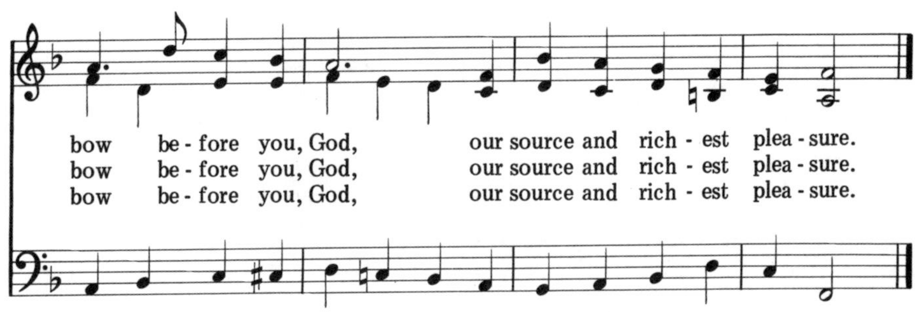

bow be - fore you, God, our source and rich - est plea - sure.
bow be - fore you, God, our source and rich - est plea - sure.
bow be - fore you, God, our source and rich - est plea - sure.

33 We Utter Our Cry

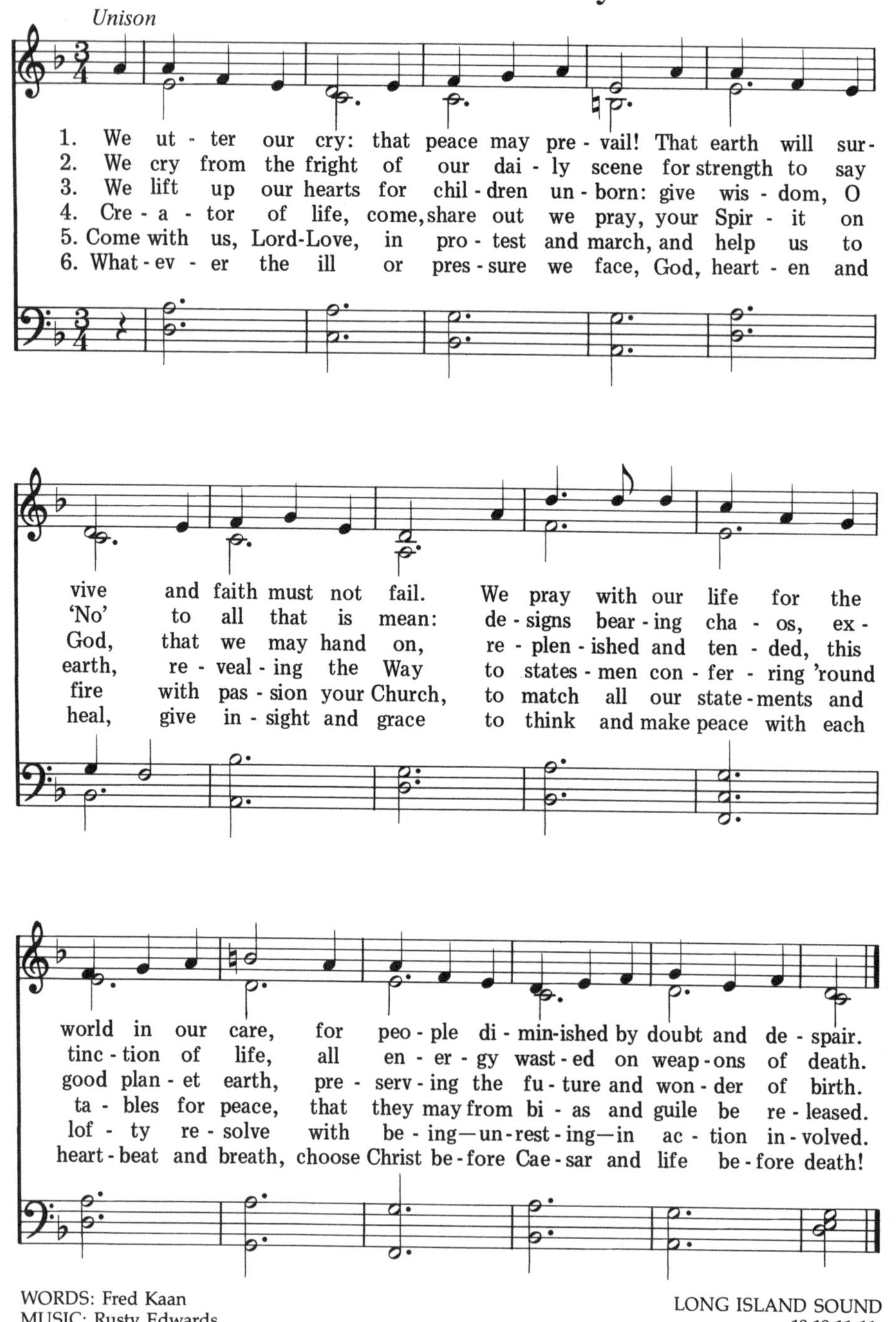

Unison
1. We ut - ter our cry: that peace may pre - vail! That earth will sur-
2. We cry from the fright of our dai - ly scene for strength to say
3. We lift up our hearts for chil - dren un - born: give wis - dom, O
4. Cre - a - tor of life, come, share out we pray, your Spir - it on
5. Come with us, Lord-Love, in pro - test and march, and help us to
6. What - ev - er the ill or pres - sure we face, God, heart - en and

vive and faith must not fail. We pray with our life for the
'No' to all that is mean: de - signs bear - ing cha - os, ex-
God, that we may hand on, re - plen - ished and ten - ded, this
earth, re - veal - ing the Way to states - men con - fer - ring 'round
fire with pas - sion your Church, to match all our state - ments and
heal, give in - sight and grace to think and make peace with each

world in our care, for peo - ple di - min-ished by doubt and de - spair.
tinc - tion of life, all en - er - gy wast - ed on weap - ons of death.
good plan - et earth, pre - serv - ing the fu - ture and won - der of birth.
ta - bles for peace, that they may from bi - as and guile be re - leased.
lof - ty re - solve with be - ing—un - rest - ing—in ac - tion in - volved.
heart - beat and breath, choose Christ be - fore Cae - sar and life be - fore death!

WORDS: Fred Kaan
MUSIC: Rusty Edwards

LONG ISLAND SOUND
10.10.11.11.

When This Child Was Born

34

Unison (or in Canon)
1. When this child was born there was cause for joy for the
2. Now we gath - er here on this hap - py morn look and
3. As The Ba - by born in a cat - tle stall came to
Lord makes each new girl and boy. Be -
see this in - fant be re - born by
earth to bless us one and all; may
hold this awe - some gift of grace. See the
wa - ter and God's sav - ing Word when the
all God's bap - tized live to bless ev - 'ry
love of God in this small face.
claim - ing of this child is heard.
neigh - bor out of grate - ful - ness.

WORDS: Rusty Edwards
MUSIC: Dale Wood

LAUREL
10.9.8.9.

35 Worship God for Saints Before Us

Unison

1. Wor - ship God for saints be - fore us; all who gave our
2. Let us greet our God with glad - ness filled with joy for
3. May the saints of faith's to - mor - row love and trust the

church its birth. They are shield - ed by God's pow - er—
faith to - day. Though not see - ing, yet be - liev - ing
God of grace. May we grow in hope - ful liv - ing

Gold has nev - er known such worth! As we now by
in the Truth, the Life, the Way. As we now by
May we know God's strong em - brace. We will still by

faith move for - ward praise the Lord of Heav'n and Earth.
faith move for - ward Christ our Lord we will o - bey.
faith move for - ward till we meet God face to face.

WORDS: Rusty Edwards
MUSIC: Dale Wood

EDEN CHURCH
8.7.8.7.8.7.

Worship, Praise, and Meditation 36

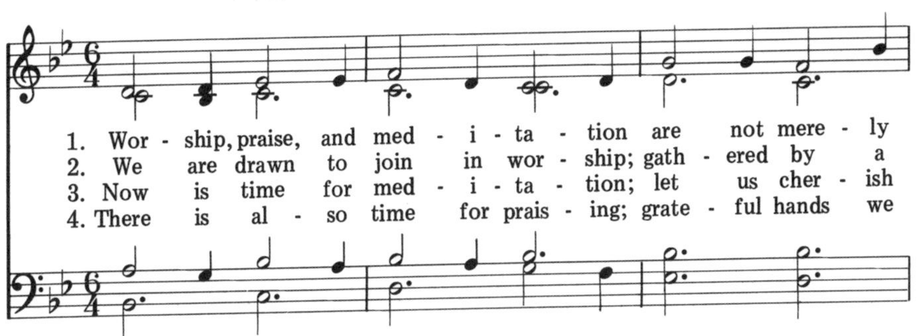

1. Wor - ship, praise, and med - i - ta - tion are not mere - ly
2. We are drawn to join in wor - ship; gath - ered by a
3. Now is time for med - i - ta - tion; let us cher - ish
4. There is al - so time for prais - ing; grate - ful hands we

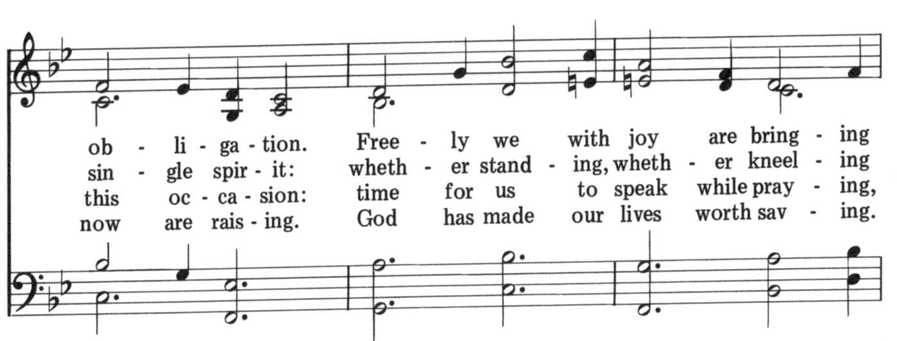

ob - li - ga - tion. Free - ly we with joy are bring - ing
sin - gle spir - it: wheth - er stand - ing, wheth - er kneel - ing
this oc - ca - sion: time for us to speak while pray - ing,
now are rais - ing. God has made our lives worth sav - ing.

all our needs and all our sing - ing.
we re - ceive an in - ner heal - ing.
time to hear what God is say - ing.
Christ up - on our hearts en - grav - ing.

WORDS and MUSIC: Rusty Edwards

BAPTISMAL LULLABY
L.M.

NOTES ON THE HYMNS

1 AS THE MOON IS TO THE SUN

Tune: *BORROWED LIGHT*   Written: Nov., 1990; Aug., 1992

Dave Brubeck helped me complete this hymn on John the Servant by suggesting ideas for the middle verse, and by writing a wonderful hymn/anthem. His wife, Iola, suggested the name *BORROWED LIGHT.*

2 BEHOLD, A WOMAN FROM THE CITY

Tune: *TEARS*   Written: January, 1983

Each time I sing this story of a city woman's sacrificial love for Jesus, I cry, so the tune is called *TEARS. TEARS* was my first published hymn tune, appearing in "The Well Woman" in April, 1983.

3 BROTHER SUN, SISTER MOON

Tune: *COREA*   Written: October, 1989

A versification that keeps to St. Francis' intent. What a joy to hear that it was sung at a conference in Assisi!

4 COME, LITTLE CHILDREN

Tune: *HOWARD*   Written: December, 1983

One of the joys of my life has been friendship with Herb Brokering. Herb and I wrote this song as a gift to my father, who is a child of God. Children of God everywhere seem to be taken by this song. Available as anthem (Harold Flammer, Inc. # E-5245).

5 FAITH IS THE YES OF THE HEART

Tune: *ROCKFORD*   Written: February, 1991

For several years, co-worker/friend Nancy Ingelson was the first to see my new hymns. I remember the day I ran upstairs to her office 20 times, as each new line of this text came. As the title implies, this text is about what faith is. Thus, we have a collection of faith images, some personal, some biblical, and two from Luther. Jane Marshall's tune, commissioned for **100 Hymns of Hope,** was the only thing on my desk when I arrived at my new office in Rockford—what a terrific welcome present. The hymn was first published in **NewSong: Brian Wren Newsletter,** May 1992.

6 FOR GOD SO LOVED THE WORLD

Tune: *THREE SIXTEEN*   Written: June, 1984

When composer Rick Drexler shared John 3:16 with me, my attitude towards God changed. This song has given me an opportunity to share the message of God's love with many children of all ages.

7 GIVE THANKS TO GOD ON HIGH

Tune: *LUDY*   Written: December, 1988

The tune was commissioned specifically for the text, and was first published in **Songs of Rejoicing.** The tune was named for Malcolm D. Ludy, my childhood pastor.

8 GOD, WE PRAISE YOU!

Tune: *ILA*   Written: February, 1983

This tune, written for my grandmother, has been published previously with several other texts, but has now found a perfect home with Chris Idle's hymn.

9 HOW LOVELY IS THY DWELLING PLACE

Tune: *COREA*   Written: August, 1989

The tune was written to reflect the psalmist's peaceful bliss in the presence of God. The unison tune is accompanied by a sparse jazz harmony using advice from composer Chick Corea: "Play only what you hear;" thus the tune name.

10 I HEAR CREATION GROANING

Tune: *FRIEDMAN*   Written: March, 1992

These days, one can almost sense creation's prayer for a new birth —a new Eden. Jane's tune was inspired by her niece, Sara, a former editor of MAD Magazine. Sara gave birth to Samuel William Friedman on the evening of Jane's mother's memorial service. Jane says that Sam's birth "was a truly joyful time as we buried one full-of-life saint and saw the life cycle complete itself in one day."

11 I WILL NOT FORGET YOU

Tune: *MOUNTAIN T.O.P.*   Written: August, 1984

This text is a paraphrase of one of my favorite Bible passages. Even when it seems that we are forsaken and forgotten, God promises to remember us. The tune is named for the Mountain Tennessee Outreach Project at Altamont.

12 IN JESUS' NAME, WE PAUSE TO PRAY

Tune: *TALLIS CANON*   Written: November, 1989

"A New Table Prayer," as it is sometimes titled, was written for a prayer retreat, led by Leanna Moen and Ron Tiedge. "Johnny Appleseed" just didn't seem to fit the occasion!

13 IN THE DARK OF EASTER MORNING

Tune: *MAGDALA*   Written: September, 1982

My first hymn tune, written at the harpsichord. I tried to capture the Elizabethan flavor of Gracia's text.

14 LAMP OF GOD UNVEILED

Tune: *LE P'ING*   Written: March, 1991

This text is an attempt to tie together several "epiphanies" in the life of Christ. It was written with the people of Epiphany Lutheran Church, Dayton, Ohio in mind.

15 LIFT YOUR VOICE REJOICING, MARY

Tune: *TALITHA CUMI*   Written: April, 1983

Talitha Cumi is an aramaic command, which means, "little girl, arise." It was written for Gracia Grindal's "There Was Jesus by the Water" (Songs of Rejoicing). While attempting to write a tune for the Charles text, it occurred that this was the right tune!

16 LORD OF FEASTING AND OF HUNGER

Tune: *CRONMILLER*   Written: March, 1986

When Vern Cronmiller visited Trinity Lutheran Church, Moline, he asked Herb and I to write a hymn for the Lutheran Church's World Hunger Appeal. Carl Schalk's anthem setting (Concordia #98-2863) enhanced the hymn.

17 LORD OF THE LIVING

Tune: *FORT WORTH*   Written: June, 1987

This tune was written during a Hymn Society sponsored hymn writing course at Texas Christian University, taught by Jaroslav Vajda and Carl Schalk.

18 LOVING SPIRIT

Tune: *BETH*   Written: July, 1990

The tune was named for Beth Cameron Edwards, who paints the most beautiful portraits I have ever seen. Shirley Erena Murray makes her pictures with words. The tune was introduced at the 1992 Hymn Society Conference at Washington, D.C.

19 NEW DAYS ARE COMING

Tune: *ANN'S ORDINATION*   Written: August, 1986

This scripture paraphrase is a glimpse of our future shalom (complete) life with God, and was a gift for fellow seminarian Ann Bergstrom.

20 NOW IT IS EVENING

Tune: *BOZEMAN*   Written: April, 1992

The tune, written specifically for "Now It Is Evening" is named for Lori Bozeman (Mountain T.O.P. staff), who taught me to love my neighbor sacrificially; loving is a privilege and an act of gratitude.

21 NOTHING IN THIS WORLD

Tune: *AGAPETOS*   Written: June, 1992

Dave Brubeck's tune and St. Paul's Epistle had been floating around my brain for a long time until they collided late one evening—a hymn was born. Sing this happy news: Jesus loves you!

22 NOW LET US FROM THIS TABLE RISE

Tune: *LORRAINE*   Written: August, 1983

This tune was a gift for my friend, bride, and spiritual guide, whose commitment to Christ and compassion for others has been an inspiration to me, and to many.

23 PRAISE THE ONE

Tune: *HULDA*   Written: June, 1986

This text is a reflection upon the profound and unique ministry of Jesus Christ, who is the source of our unity in mission. The tune is by the distinguished organist Paul Manz, who became so intrigued with the text that he claims the tune wrote itself.

24 PRINCES, PAUPERS, ROYAL CHILDREN

Tune: *ROCK ISLAND*   Written: October, 1988

The tune was commissioned by South Park Presbyterian Church and St. John's Lutheran Church, both located in Rock Island, Illinois, thus the tune name.

25 REJOICE AND PREPARE NOW

Tune: *RESTORATION*   Written: September 1985; revised, 1992

The words of preparation from Isaiah begin, "comfort my people," but we tend to turn Advent into a season that is anything but comforting. Prepare for the rescuer, and bring out the trumpets! The text was written with *ST. DENIO* in mind, but I am wild about Ronald Watson's new tune.

26 SMALL THINGS COUNT

Tune: *BENJAMIN'S SWING*   Written: February, 1987

Shirley's new text is simply profound (profoundly simple!). One of the small things that count for me is improvising new words, rhythms, and melodies with my son Benjamin as I push him on the swing!

27 THE DESERT SHALL REJOICE

Tune: *ADVENT ROSE*   Written: December, 1982

This early tune was inspired by Gracia's Isaiah paraphrase. It was showcased at the Lutheran Festival of Worship and Witness at Minneapolis in 1983.

28 THE GREATEST LOVE OF ALL

Tune: *VALENTINE* Tune Written: October, 1984
Words Written: February, 1992

The love of God is stronger than any other love. The hymn was a Valentine's Day gift to my wife, Lori.

29 TO A MAID ENGAGED TO JOSEPH

Tune: *ANNUNCIATION* Written: November, 1982

Gracia and I wrote twenty hymns together during my seminary years. This hymn was stylistically a follow-up to the first hymn we wrote together, "In the Dark of Easter Morning". We are both grateful that it seems to have become an accepted carol of the season. The day it was written, Gracia and I both had laryngitis, so this hymn was first "sung" by an alto recorder and a guitar with one string!

30 TWO PEOPLE

Tune: *ERMUNTRE DICH* Written: December, 1989

"Two People" includes a theology of marriage, and echoes of both the traditional vows and the frequently read First Corinthians passage.

31 WE ALL ARE ONE IN MISSION

Tune: *ACCORD* Written: August, 1985

Jack L. Ralston (of CBN University) wrote this in "The Hymn": "Dr. Edwards' new hymn on missions is fitted to the music of *LANCASHIRE*, providing a sturdy and stirring call to serve Christ." It was sung at gatherings of over a dozen denominations and selected for four hymnals before it had its own tune, *ACCORD*. Dale Wood's new tune, available also in anthem form, is outstanding, and gives the hymn its full power.

32 WE BOW BEFORE YOU, GOD

Tune: *EPHESIAN*   Written: January, 1985

Text and tune were written by request for a convention of the American Lutheran Church. The triplets allow the words to be sung as they are said.

33 WE UTTER OUR CRY

Tune: *LONG ISLAND SOUND*   Written: April, 1989

The tune was written at the Mercy Center, Madison, Connecticut, while I was working on my doctoral project. Composed specifically for these words, it reflects the text's longing for peace. The unresolved final chord is a reminder that peacemaking is unfinished business.

34 WHEN THIS CHILD WAS BORN

Tune: *LAUREL*   Written: December, 1990

This text was written for the baptism of an awesome gift of grace, my son, Ian Christopher Edwards, whose sponsors were Christopher and Leanna Moen. Dale Wood suggested that we submit the words for publication with his tune *LAUREL*.

35 WORSHIP GOD FOR SAINTS BEFORE US

Tune: *EDEN CHURCH*   Written: January, 1990

The text was commissioned by Faith Lutheran Church, Moline, Illinois for their 40th anniversary, specifically for Dale Wood's tune.

36 WORSHIP, PRAISE, AND MEDITATION

Tune: *BAPTISMAL LULLABY*   Tune Written: November, 1987
                           Words Written: June, 1988

The tune was originally written for Jaroslav J. Vajda's text, "See This Wonder in the Making," and was published for the baptism of my son (and pal), Benjamin Ganz Edwards. Benjamin's sponsors were Bob and Julie Blew and Ron Tiedge. The text, a celebration of the various expressions of worship, was written almost a year later.

CONTRIBUTORS

Herbert F. Brokering, Minnesota

Dave Brubeck, Connecticut

Carl P. Daw, Jr., Connecticut

Timothy Dudley-Smith, England

Fred Pratt Green, England

Gracia Grindal, Minnesota

Christopher Idle, England

Fred Kaan, England

Paul Manz, Illinois

Jane Marshall, Texas

Shirley Erena Murray, New Zealand

Carl Schalk, Illinois

Robert Sterling, Texas

Ronald Watson, England

Dale Wood, California

INDEX OF SCRIPTURAL ALLUSIONS

ALPHABETICAL INDEX OF HYMN TUNES

METRICAL INDEX OF HYMN TUNES

TOPICAL INDEX OF HYMNS

*Some churches now use a three year lectionary for weekly Scripture readings.
"2 ADVENT B' refers to the second Sunday in Advent, year B (two).

ALPHABETICAL INDEX OF FIRST LINES